S0-BJF-748

Birchtown

AND THE BLACK LOYALIST EXPERIENCE FROM 1775 TO THE PRESENT

Birchtown

AND THE BLACK LOYALIST EXPERIENCE FROM 1775 TO THE PRESENT

STEPHEN DAVIDSON

PHOTOGRAPHY BY PETER ZWICKER

FORMAC PUBLISHING COMPANY LIMITED
HALIFAX

Text Copyright © 2019 by Stephen Davidson
Images Copyright © 2019 by Formac Publishing Company Ltd.

All rights reserved. No part of this book may be reproduced or transmitted in any form or by any means, electronic or mechanical, including photocopying, or by any information storage or retrieval system, without permission in writing from the publisher.

Formac Publishing Company Limited recognizes the support of the Province of Nova Scotia through the Department of Communities, Culture and Heritage. We are pleased to work in partnership with the Province of Nova Scotia to develop and promote our cultural resources for all Nova Scotians. We acknowledge the support of the Canada Council for the Arts, which last year invested $153 million to bring the arts to Canadians throughout the country. This project has been made possible in part by the Government of Canada.

Cover design: Tyler Cleroux
Cover images: Peter Zwicker, Tourism Nova Scotia,
Black Loyalist Heritage Centre, Black Loyalist Heritage Society

Library and Archives Canada Cataloguing in Publication

Title: Birchtown and the Black Loyalist experience : from 1775 to the present / Stephen Davidson ; photography by Peter Zwicker.

Names: Davidson, Stephen Eric, 1953- author. | Zwicker, Peter, photographer.

Description: Includes bibliographical references and index.

Identifiers: Canadiana 2019004795X | ISBN 9781459505568 (softcover)

Subjects: LCSH: Blacks—Nova Scotia—Birchtown—History. | LCSH: African Americans—Nova Scotia— Birchtown—History. | LCSH: Birchtown (N.S.)—History. | LCSH: African American loyalists—Nova Scotia—Birchtown—History. | CSH: Black loyalists—Nova Scotia—Birchtown—History.

Classification: LCC FC2349.B56 D38 2019 | DDC 971.6/2500496—dc23

Formac Publishing Company Limited
5502 Atlantic Street
Halifax, Nova Scotia, Canada
B3H 1G4
www.formac.ca

Printed and bound in Canada

CONTENTS

Foreword
BLACK LOYALISTS AND HISTORY'S FORGOTTEN EMANCIPATION
· · · · · ·

Most North Americans think of the Underground Railroad when they hear of enslaved Africans fleeing their masters to find sanctuary outside of the United States. Gaining its name from the safe houses ("stations") and secret routes ("rail lines") provided by abolitionists, this clandestine network began as early as 1831 when a slave owner complained that "an underground railroad" had helped one of his slaves escape to Ohio. More than 100,000 people escaped slavery during the years that the "railroad" was in operation.

But enslaved Blacks had followed the North Star to freedom before the Underground Railroad's inauguration. The greatest emancipation of enslaved Africans before the nineteenth century began in 1775. By 1783, upwards of twenty thousand Black men, women and children had run away from their Patriot masters during the course of the American Revolution. Of these, eight to ten thousand survived the war and left the United States as free people. These emancipated Africans became known as Black Loyalists.

Five thousand Black Loyalists found sanctuary in Great Britain, the country that had emancipated them. Seeking climates similar to the southern colonies or deciding to remain with their military regiments, others migrated to the German states, Belgium, the West Indies and the Bahamas. Black Loyalists were among the first settlers of Australia's Botany Bay in 1788. Four years later, almost two thousand Black Loyalists founded the colony of Sierra Leone in Western Africa.

At least 3,500 Black Loyalists found refuge in Nova Scotia, sailing north in evacuation fleets from New York City in 1783. Thousands more undocumented refugees also left Savannah, Georgia, Charleston, South Carolina, St. Augustine, East Florida and other ports between 1782 and 1784. Scores of Black Loyalists journeyed overland to settle in what is now Ontario and Quebec.

Despite their numbers and the breadth of their dispersal, Black Loyalists have not received the attention that their history deserves. Loyalists — whether white or Black — were dismissed in American historical accounts as traitors, insignificant in number and impact. Canadian histories ignored a minority within the Maritimes that did not wield economic or cultural influence. The oral history of Black Loyalist descendants kept their ancestors' story alive until it was brought to the attention of the larger community with the establishment of the Black Cultural Centre in Cherry Brook, Nova Scotia. Established in 1983 to preserve and promote the heritage of African Nova Scotians, the centre is both a museum and cultural gathering place.

The Black Loyalist Heritage Centre in Birchtown, Nova Scotia, opened thirty-two years later, in 2015. The heritage centre is dedicated to celebrating the history of Canada's Black Loyalist founders.

Part One
THE HISTORIC BIRCHTOWN SITE

The windows of the Black Loyalist Heritage Centre reflect an image of St. Paul's Church, which once housed a congregation of Black Loyalist descendants. The church is one stop along Birchtown's historic walking trail.

The National Monument
CELEBRATING THE RECOGNITION OF HERITAGE

Unveiled on July 20, 1996, the plaque commissioned by the National Historic Sites and Monuments Board commemorates the story of the Black Loyalists at Birchtown *in just eighty-eight words.*

"After the American Revolution, over 3500 free African Americans loyal to the Crown moved to Nova Scotia and New Brunswick where they established the first Black communities in Canada. Birchtown, founded in 1783, was the largest and most influential of these settlements. The population declined in 1792 when many Black Loyalists, frus-

BELOW: Had it not been for the efforts of the Black Loyalists' descendants, this beautiful vista would have become the site of a provincial landfill.

RIGHT: Once a burial ground for the community, the land that overlooks Birchtown Bay is now the site of the national monument to the men and women who founded Birchtown.

trated by their treatment in the Maritimes, immigrated to Sierra Leone in West Africa. Although diminished in numbers, Birchtown remains a proud symbol of the struggle by Blacks in the Maritimes and elsewhere for justice and dignity."

The founders of Birchtown — men and women who had been emancipated by the British government — gave the settlement its name. Because documents that certified their status as free people bore the signature of General Samuel Birch, the British commandant of New York City, they were known as Birch certificates. The name "Birchtown" celebrated the fact that its settlers were no longer enslaved.

Given the richness of this heritage — revealed through primary documents, archaeological digs and painstaking research — it is astounding to think that just a century ago very little of the Black Loyalist story was known to mainstream Nova Scotia, or Canada.

The entry for "Birchtown" in a 1922 book entitled *The Place Names of the Province of Nova Scotia* demonstrates how much knowledge of Black Loyalists had been lost since they came to the Maritimes:

The interpretive plaque has at its centre a "Birch Certificate," the document that verified each Black Loyalist's freedom.
Celebrating their emancipation, the settlers named their community Birchtown.

"*BIRCHTOWN: A descriptive name, as the birch wood was plentiful there. This place is opposite Shelburne town. It was laid out about the year 1783 as a town for the Negroes. They numbered about four thousand at the time and built quite a large town there. The greater number of them were removed to Sierra Leone in 1790 or 1791.*"

Things were no better by the mid-twentieth century. In 1963, Black Loyalist descendants wrote to the Nova Scotia Historic Sites Advisory Board to seek recognition of the town's significance, documenting the lack of understanding of Birchtown's history and exhibiting an unself-conscious racism common at the time. The board's chair advised the premier of the day that Birchtown was only "a sort of shack town, a settlement of the slaves who came with the loyalists and were left there by the loyalists who moved on." Black Loyalists, he felt, were not important enough to be considered historic.

Were it not for the tireless efforts of the Shelburne County Cultural Awareness Society (now the Black Loyalist Heritage Society) that formed in 1991, Birchtown might well have been made into a landfill site and bulldozed into oblivion — an act that would have been tantamount to burying the history of one of Nova Scotia's founding peoples. In 1994, the society finally had the landing site of Black Loyalists recognized as having historical importance for all Canadians via a successful application to the Historic Sites and Monuments Board of Canada.

Black Loyalists

Black Loyalists — In the latter part of the twentieth century, historians began to use this term to describe Blacks who supported Great Britain during the American Revolution. In the eighteenth century, these people of African descent who had been enslaved by Patriot masters and emancipated by the British were simply known as "the black refugees" or "the free blacks." At the Black Loyalist Heritage Centre, the term "Black Loyalist" is used to include those who were enslaved by white Loyalists and thus were part of the general Loyalist diaspora.

The Black Loyalist Burial Ground
THE LOST GRAVES THAT SAVED BIRCHTOWN

Despite the lack of tombstones or written records, the community's oral history indicates that the land near the bay had once been Birchtown's graveyard. Historical deeds made a brief mention of "the burial ground" because it bordered two

BLACK BURIAL GROUND

Legend and oral history told that this piece of land was a burial ground for Blacks. There is no formal record of the burial ground, though historical deeds from two adjoining plots of land show that the properties border on "the burial ground". Families in the area remember being told not to play on the site, because it was sacred ground.

There are no records as to who may be buried on the site, though one church record suggests that a man named John Stevens, who died in the 1800's, was buried "on the northwestern side of Shelburne Harbour", most likely in Birchtown. Unfortunately, most of the old church records were destroyed in a house fire.

The burial ground is the first piece of property the Black Loyalist Heritage Society obtained. In 1996, it was recognized with a plaque from the National Historic Sites and Monuments Board of Canada. The Black Loyalist Heritage Society has constructed a retaining wall to protect the site from further water erosion The Iron Gates located at the entrance of the grounds were donated by Dr. Clifford "Nick" Skinner of the New Brunswick Black Loyalist Society.

TOP: *A portion of this stoneware mug was the first object to be uncovered in the initial 1993 archaeological dig. This discovery prompted archaeologists to launch further excavations in search of Birchtown's lost history.*

LEFT: *The oral history of Birchtown remembers this land as the burial ground for the community's original settlers.*

adjoining plots of land. Senior community members share stories of being told as children that they were not to play on the site because it was sacred ground.

The disappearance of Black Loyalist graves is common throughout the Maritimes. Not having the resources to buy tombstones or hire engravers, Blacks and poor whites marked the resting places of their dead with homemade wooden crosses that slowly decayed. In larger settlements where Black Loyalists were buried in the community graveyard, they were interred at the back of the burial grounds, far from white Loyalists.

In 1992, the Shelburne area was in need of a new garbage dump site. There were already ninety landfills in Nova Scotia located on or near Black communities. Little wonder, then, that when white developers proposed a new dump site for Shelburne, they planned to situate it in a hamlet of 221 Black people — Birchtown. Besides the negative impact of the landfill on the local community, the use of heavy construction equipment and the creation of an access road would have destroyed sites that might provide scholars with valuable clues to the history of Birchtown. The "sacred ground" itself would be as lost as the names of those buried there.

Descendants of the original Black Loyalist settlers filed papers with the Nova Scotia Human Rights Commission to have the landfill project halted. Beyond the charge that this was yet another example of environmental racism, the community also wanted to demonstrate that, on its merits, Birchtown was worth preserving as a historic site.

Written records offered only minimal details of the community's early history. To determine the significance of Birchtown, another type of record had to be consulted — the complete and unbiased evidence contained in the ground itself. The director of the Nova Scotia Human Rights Commission approached the archaeology unit at St. Mary's University in Halifax to have the area assessed for its historical significance. But where to begin?

In the fall of 1993, archaeologists Laird Niven and Stephen Powell surveyed the village site to determine the best starting point to unearth Birchtown's hidden history. A shallow depression — something that indicated human activity rather than a natural formation — was a promising discovery. With the first shovel test, a piece of dot-patterned stoneware emerged. A second dig turned up a clay pipe stem and some refined earthenware.

These discoveries were enough to warrant a further investigation, and Niven returned with Stephen Davis in the following year to conduct a more extensive excavation. Over time, 16,000 artifacts from the late 1700s came to light. The ground had begun to speak of Birchtown's forgotten history.

A white clay pipe discarded over two hundred years ago was the second artifact discovered at Birchtown.

St. Paul's Church
Celebrating a Heritage of Faith

Through the darkest days of slavery, service to the Crown and settlement in British North America, the faith of the Black Loyalists sustained them with hope for the future.

St. Paul's Church was built 105 years after the arrival of the Black Loyalists, on land donated by Enoch Scott, a Black fisherman. Repurposed as an Anglican church in 1906, St. Paul's had a congregation comprised of fifty-four families. Black Loyalist descendants with the names of Shepherd,

Warrington, Scott and Herbert worshipped there until the church closed in 1989. Upon its de-consecration in 2007, the Black Loyalist Heritage Society acquired St. Paul's to serve as a memorial to the faith heritage of Birchtown's founders.

St. Paul's Church is a reminder of the many thriving congregations that once gathered for worship in Birchtown. Both the Methodists and Baptists had vibrant leaders who also visited other Black Loyalist communities to preach.

St. Paul's sanctuary includes elements of the early English style of church architecture comprising tall, narrow lancet windows with their characteristic pointed arches. The Black Loyalist Heritage Society had the three stained glass windows on the back wall of St. Paul's sanctuary restored in 2010.

"Whenever we view the light shining through these stained-glass prisms, we'll see refracted the beautiful hues of the Birchtown Mosaic — a people who have made the effort to pay homage to the ideals our collective ancestors shed their blood, sweat and tears for."

Deborah Davis Hill, Ethno-historian

No longer used as a place of worship, the historic church is now a venue for community gatherings, historical re-enactments, concerts and weddings.

The earliest places of worship for Black Loyalists who arrived in the Shelburne area in 1783 were woodland clearings or riversides. During their days of enslavement, Blacks had sought out such sheltered areas for their religious services, far from the prying eyes of whites. Here, both free and enslaved blacks gathered to hear the sermons of Black Loyalist preachers such as David George, Moses Wilkinson, Boston King and John Marrant.

OPPOSITE PAGE: St. Paul's served Birchtown as an Anglican house of worship from 1906 to 1989.

THIS PAGE: The early churches of Birchtown also served as town halls. In the fall of 1791, British abolitionist John Clarkson spoke to a crowd of over three hundred Black Loyalists who had gathered in the Methodist Church to offer them free passage to Sierra Leone.

Literary Impact of Black Loyalist Ministers

John Marrant *A Narrative of the Lord's Wonderful Dealings,* is less important for its accomplishments than for its influence upon historical and literary trends among Black people in North America and in Africa. His was a message of perseverance, a testimony to the success a Black man and a Christian could achieve through faith in God and in himself, and his served as a model for generations of Black American writers."David George's *An Account of the Life of Mr. David George, from Sierra Leone in Africa Boston King Memoirs of the Life of Boston King*" was published in a British magazine in 1798.

Visitors to the Black Loyalist Heritage Centre have the opportunity to experience the terrain of Birchtown in the 1780s by following a historical trail around the site.

Aminata's Walk
CELEBRATING JOURNEYS

Today, visitors are asked to imagine the reaction of Birchtown's first settlers as they approached these woods.

While the Black Loyalist Heritage Centre commemorates the contributions of important historical features, it also recognizes Birchtown's most famous fictional character, Aminata Diallo. The walking trail that encircles the heritage centre is named in her honour, reminding visitors of the Black Loyalists' long journey to freedom and their settlement in Nova Scotia.

Birchtown Bay once provided a means for vessels to arrive at the Black Loyalist settlement. The bay is an arm of Shelburne Harbour, which was once regarded as one of the best in Nova Scotia.

Aminata is the heroine of Lawrence Hill's 2007 novel (and subsequent television mini-series), *The Book of Negroes*. In the novel, Aminata is kidnapped in her native Niger, is enslaved in the American south, finds refuge in New York City, settles in Birchtown, sails for Sierra Leone and ends her life's journey in Great Britain. Aminata's fictional life mirrors the biographies of thousands of actual Black Loyalists.

As visitors make their way along the forested trail, they have an opportunity to reflect on all the hopes that Birchtown's Black founders would have had as they first explored the woods and streams of their new settlement. In late 1783, the settlers would have looked over the terrain for features that would support their particular occupations. Where could a blacksmith build his forge? Would the nearby streams provide sufficient power for a miller's needs? How difficult would it be to construct wharves for the fishermen? And perhaps most importantly, what grants of land would be theirs, demonstrating in no uncertain terms that they were indeed a free people?

TOP: Providing visitors with an impression of the clothing of Birchtown's first settlers, historical re-enactors also recount stories of Birchtown's early decades.

LEFT: Safe or poisonous? Being unfamiliar with Nova Scotia's plants and animals, the Black Loyalists would learn about the resources of their new home from the Mi'kmaq, the province's Indigenous people.

Traditionally, Black Loyalists who found work in nearby Shelburne would walk seven kilometres through the forest.

The Pit House
CELEBRATING SURVIVAL AND INGENUITY

The Loyalist refugees who settled around Shelburne Harbour lived in tents, log cabins, unfinished cellars or on ships until houses could be constructed. Birchtown is unique in that its settlers constructed small shelters known as pit houses.

A short walk into the forest brings the visitor to a replica of what archaeologists describe as a "pit house." Constructed out of readily available materials, such pit houses sheltered many Black Loyalists during their first winter in Birchtown.

Building homes over the summer and early fall of 1783 was a challenge for both the white and Black Loyalists who settled along the shores of Shelburne's razor-shaped harbour. Some of the white settlers who arrived in the fall lived on board their evacuation ships until the spring; others stayed on shore in temporary huts. Some spent the winter in the cellars of their unfinished houses while others lived above ground in old British army tents.

For Black settlers, it was a different story. Beyond a reliance on crude huts and canvas tents, historical records and archaeology have until recently shed very little light on how over a thousand Black Loyalists survived their first winter of freedom. It was a miserable existence in substandard conditions beyond what any government should have allowed humans to endure — especially those who pledged allegiance to the Crown. In the 1930s, John Farmer, a descendant of a man enslaved by Loyalists, told Nova Scotian writer Clara Dennis more about pit houses. Dennis could not believe that anyone had once lived in "holes in the ground."

Whether early settlers' homes were constructed by Black or white Loyalists, moss and earth were typical materials for filling in the gaps between log walls and roofs made of slender trunks.

Having been responsible for building temporary shelters for the British Army during the American Revolution, some Black Loyalists used those rudimentary structures as their models, and built pit houses to see them through the winter.

Archaeological evidence suggests that some of these cubic-metre pit houses remained the homes of Birchtown's settlers for years.

"That's all they ever were," said Farmer. "I've heard my grandfather tell about them. The government gave the Negroes land there, but they had no houses, not even log cabins. They just dug a hole in the ground and put a little peaked roof over it. They chose a hill for their purpose because the ground was drier. The peak roof would shed the water when it rained. There was a small trapdoor in one side of the roof and the Negroes entered the house by dropping right down through. And that was the Black man's home — a hole in the ground with a roof over the hole."

Sixty years later, archaeologist Laird Niven excavated a shelter such as Farmer described. It was a depression measuring 1.5 metres by 1.5 metres and was about half a metre deep. Although this "pit house" was built as a temporary measure, the evidence Niven discovered suggests that some were used for more than one year.

The pit houses that Black Loyalists used to provide shelter through the winter may have been inspired by similar structures built by the British Army on its marches during the American Revolution. Given that many of Birchtown's settlers had once been members of the Black Pioneers, a company responsible for building support structures for the king's army, they would have had a great deal of experience in building such shelters. To date, Birchtown is the only Black Loyalist settlement in Atlantic Canada in which such pit houses have been discovered.

PIT HOUSE

With a mix of *unsettle* being *displaced* in 1783, the *British* government in *the 1780s and* tried *various* of *settlers* and *gave* many *immigrants land* and *supplies*. As *settlers* were *still* very *in* these *conditions* they *unable* to *survive the* *land* and *therefore received smaller* *plots*.

With no *aid* to *call* their *own,* *many black Loyalists* had to *face* their *new homelands*. *It* was *cold,* *worse affected winter.* *In* order *to survive* they *dug out houses such as this* *one.* *Black settlers* were *dug in the ground,* *with a shelter fashioned out* *of free* *these built.* *It* *sufficient in her resources mass and strength that they managed to* *survive* *this holds their* *need to national dwelling.* *Archaeologists discovered*

The Old Schoolhouse Museum
CELEBRATING THE VALUE OF EDUCATION

Education, as symbolized by the Birchtown schoolhouse, was highly valued by the Black Loyalists. Within two years of the town's founding, Stephen Blucke became its first teacher.

Sponsored by the Associates of Dr. Bray, an English philanthropic organization, Birchtown's first school opened in 1785 with Colonel Stephen Blucke as its teacher. Classes convened in the Methodist Meeting House where St. Paul's Church now stands. The local inspector was impressed by Blucke's conduct and efficient management — and by the satisfactory progress of the school's original thirty-six students. Charles Inglis, the Anglican bishop for Nova Scotia, felt that Black Loyalist children were better served than the five hundred white children in Shelburne whose parents could not afford to pay tuition to any of that town's twelve white schools. Following the exodus to Sierra Leone, Blucke saw his student numbers dwindle to just fourteen, forcing him to close Birchtown's first school in September of 1795.

Roswell Brown, a white schoolmaster who had emigrated from Albany, New York, later re-established Birchtown's school with the help of the Church of England. The present one-room schoolhouse was constructed in the 1830s, fifty

ABOVE: An old school desk from the nineteenth century reminds visitors that this schoolhouse was built fifty years after the arrival of the Black Loyalists.

RIGHT: As the oldest building on the Birchtown site, the schoolhouse served as the community's interpretive museum until the construction of the Black Loyalist Heritage Centre in 2015.

Exhibits of African artifacts provide visitors with an understanding that was not celebrated in an earlier era's textbooks. Such cultural objects and crafts would have amazed and inspired the students who once attended the Birchtown school.

Exhibits in the schoolhouse remind visitors of all that Africans and their descendants lost during enslavement in America. As these chains demonstrate, Black Loyalists were once considered property.

Depending on the colony where an African was enslaved or the severity of the white enslaver, a metal stand such as this may have been used to restrain or punish those who tried to escape.

years after the arrival of Black Loyalists, and is noteworthy for being one of Nova Scotia's first integrated schools.

The Birchtown schoolhouse serves as a reminder of how much Black Loyalists valued the opportunity to learn the skills that would equip them for life in Nova Scotia. Acquiring an education was, however, an ongoing struggle. Often, neighbouring white communities would forbid the teaching of mathematics, reading and writing. They wanted to keep Black Loyalists as a source of cheap, illiterate labour. Despite this opposition, between 1785 and 1791 approximately three to four hundred Black Loyalist children were attending schools in Nova Scotia's five major Black communities. Their teachers were shaping the next generation, providing them with the skills they would need to rise above the disadvantages their parents had known as enslaved people.

Artifacts of Birchtown's Early Days

The artifacts displayed in the exhibition hall in Birchtown are a combination of objects that Black Loyalist settlers would have brought with them from their time in New York City and the British wares that they purchased from stores in nearby Shelburne.

Most of the artifacts were found at what is identified as the Acker site — what may have been the home of Stephen and Margaret Blucke. While their neighbours were labourers, fishermen and subsistence farmers, the Bluckes were the only couple in Birchtown that could be described as members of the middle class. Archaeologists discovered 13,000 artifacts in Birchtown, some of which are on display at the Black Loyalist Heritage Centre.

One midden (garbage disposal area) excavated by archaeologists at the Acker site initially revealed creamware, glass and nails. When more rocks were removed, they found a porcelain rim, a bottle fragment and the base of a tumbler.

A second midden contained dark green bottle glass, leaded glass, slipware, agateware and Anglo-American coarse earthenware. Dating of the artifacts shows that they were made around the year 1778, which coincides with the period of the community's founding. (These items would have been brought to Nova Scotia in 1783.)

The pattern of artifacts found at Birchtown shows a similarity to eighteenth century slave sites in the southeastern United States — the home colonies for most of Birchtown's settlers. In other words, the pattern of the kinds of artifacts found in Birchtown is one that is common to Africans who were once enslaved. This is the first evidence found in Nova Scotia to show such a parallel.

These chains were once used to bind enslaved Africans.

One of the period pieces used in the television mini-series
The Book of Negroes. *Note the lack of decoration and colour.*
Until the early nineteenth century, men typically wore knee
breeches — short trousers fastened at or just below the knee.

A costume for the television mini-series, this coat and scarf
ensemble demonstrate the heaviness of clothing for inclement
weather — and the fact that it was not waterproof.

This blue hand-painted pearlware saucer has a Chinese-influenced motif. (an Acker site artifact)

This bottle may have contained a single dose of medicine. It may indicate that Shelburne had a Loyalist-era pharmacy. (an Acker site artifact)

Hand-painted, underglaze blue pearlware cups such as this were produced in bulk in England and exported to many British colonies in the late eighteenth century. (an Acker site artifact)

This simple musical instrument provided a bit of entertainment. (an Acker site artifact)

Know your Pottery

Earthenware is pottery created at temperatures below the point of vitrification, preventing it from attaining glass-like qualities. Porcelain, bone china and stoneware are all examples of vitreous (glass-like) pottery. The most ancient of pottery types, earthenware has to be glazed to be watertight.

Slipware is pottery made using "slip" (a liquid mixture of clay or other materials suspended in water) to decorate a piece of pottery before it is fired.

Creamware is pottery that has a lead glaze over a pale body that was developed by Josiah Wedgwood, the famous English potter, around 1750. About thirty years later, Wedgwood was able to change its cream colour to a bluish shade of white. This new pottery was known as pearlware.

Agateware is pottery decorated with contrasting coloured clays. It was made in England between 1725 and 1750.

Broken glass tumbler/diamond pattern. From Acker site, belonging to a family with great means

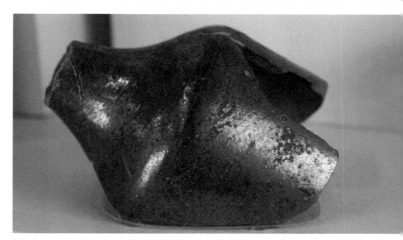

This is the shoulder and neck portion of an English brown stoneware bottle. At the time of the Acker site, it would have likely contained a beverage.

A young girl likely used this small brass thimble as she learned to sew — a skill that was part of the curriculum for girls at Black Loyalist schools. (an Acker site artifact)

Three cannons on a button indicate the British Royal Artillery. The particular way in which the cannons were represented changed from time to time. A number of Birchtown's settlers had once served in this department.

Imported hand-painted pearlware saucers were part of everyday tableware. This particular palate of colours was common from the late 1770s to about 1830. (an Acker site artifact)

This type of refined earthenware ceramic is called creamware. The shape and rim of this vessel suggests use as a chamber pot — an item usually stored under the bed. It was used as an alternative to visiting the outhouse at night or during inclement weather. (an Acker site artifact)

This earthenware bowl or jug was made for kitchen use. It is similar in design and manufacture to earthenware utensils known to have been made in colonial America by people of African descent. It is the only one of its kind found at the Acker site. As yet, it has not been linked to a specific craft tradition.

This is an English gunflint from the Acker site. Situated in the hammer of a musket's flintlock mechanism, it struck a piece of steel called a frizzen to create a spark. That in turn ignited the gunpowder that caused the musket to fire. The discovery of the flint indicates that the person living on the Acker site owned a musket.

This artifact is a beautiful example of an early transfer-printed bowl. The willow pattern was highly favoured by English ceramic manufacturers. It remains widely available to this day. Such a bowl indicates that the owners expected to entertain guests in their home. (an Acker site artifact)

Part Two
Black Loyalist History

Looking more like water than glass, the floor of the Black Loyalist Heritage Centre reminds visitors of the epic sea journey that free Blacks made to Nova Scotia at the close of the American Revolution.

Black Loyalists
THEIR LOST AFRICAN HERITAGE

African masks traditionally represented the spirit of the ancestors inhabitating the wearer.

Canadians of European descent can usually identify their country of origin and celebrate aspects of their ancestors' culture and history. For Canadians of African descent whose ancestors who were the victims of slavery, family ties had been severed, making it difficult to trace ancestral origins, language and many traditions.

Those who had been enslaved just prior to the American Revolution experienced a geographical separation from their countries of origin, but many managed to hang on to aspects of language, music and traditions in the New World. Subsequent generations of those enslaved people grew further separated from their African roots through continued loss of their native language, the denial of education and ongoing separation from their ethnic groups.

Within the *Book of Negroes* ledger there are hints of what little African heritage the Black Loyalists were able to retain. For just a handful, keeping their African names was a way to hold on to their heritage. Only 1 per cent of the male names listed in the British ledger are African in origin. None of the female names indicate an African heritage. Despite misspellings, scholars have been able to identify names common to the Akan culture of Ghana: there was one Black Loyalist named Quaco (Kwaku), two were Cudjoe (Kwado), one was Quamina (Kwamena), three were Quash (Kwasi) and nine were Cuffie (Kofi). (Interestingly, a Cuffy Cummings became the head of a Birchtown family. Would they have known the Ghanaian origin of their ancestor's name?)

Five listed in the *Book of Negroes* ledger knew that they were born in Africa (sometimes calling it Guinea). Isaac Anderson, a Birchtown settler who applied to go to Sierra Leone, identified Angola as his birthplace. These five may have been able to tell their children of a homeland far away. Within two years of Richard Wheeler's arrival in what is now New Brunswick, the Black Loyalist was using Corankapone, his African name, when making petitions to the colonial government.

Kente cloth, a traditional textile of West African nations. The piece shown here is a type of silk and cotton fabric made of interwoven cloth strips.

A ceremonial pendant by the Oba people of West Africa. It is thought to show the mother of Oba Esigle, the ruler of Benin in the 16th century. The heads along the top of the face represent the Portuguese, symbolizing Benin's alliance with and control over Europeans.

A djembe drum, illustrating music of West Africa. Music was one of the few things that couldn't be stripped from the enslaved Africans in the new world.

For people of African descent, music is intrinsic to their culture. The djembe, a drum traditionally seen as sacred, was used in rituals, worship and for healing ceremonies. Close to a hundred Black Loyalists served as field drummers in a variety of German and British regiments during the American Revolution.

Except for what survived in the oral histories passed down from generation to generation, the Black Loyalists who found sanctuary in the Maritime Provinces were people who had been stripped of their African heritage. DNA testing is now able to connect twenty-first century Canadians to specific regions of Africa, providing a link that written history has denied them. But the settlers of Birchtown would have had no opportunity to learn about their African homeland or other aspects of their heritage, which are now spotlighted at the Black Loyalist Heritage Centre.

Those enslaved to work in the New World were captured along the coast of West and West Central Africa, areas that today contain the countries of Senegal, Gambia, Guinea, Sierra Leone, Liberia, Ivory Coast, Ghana, Togo, Benin, Nigeria, Cameroon, Equatorial Guinea, Mali, Gabon, Congo, Democratic Republic of Congo and Angola. These ancestral lands of Black Loyalists gave rise to some of Africa's greatest empires and most renowned works of art.

Flourishing for over 1,300 years, the Noks of northern Nigeria were noted for the creation of life-sized terra cotta sculptures. As early as 900 CE, the Igbo-Ukwu people developed metalworking technology, specializing in bronze work. The Asante of central Ghana were known for their crafts, garments, kente cloth and sculptures. Ancient Ghana had dominated West Africa's trade in gold and salt.

As with the histories of Asian and European kingdoms, West Africa experienced a series of influential empires, each with its "golden age." The Malians supplanted the Ghanaian Empire in 1235. Gao, Djenne and Timbuktu became major centres of Mali trade and learning. Timbuktu, the City of Books, was home to the University of Sankore, a Muslim centre of learning that was founded in 989 CE. The Songhai rose up, surpassing

Bronze pendant of a male face with scarification patterns.
The Igbo people of Nigeria had similar patterns on their faces
as a sign of power and status.

This terra cotta statue was created by the Nok people
of Nigeria in the 6th century BCE. It illustrates the
sophistication of West African art.

the Mali Empire in wealth, area and power until their
defeat in 1591. Stepping into the power vacuum, the
Benin (or Edo) Empire began trading a variety of goods
with the Portuguese. Located in modern Nigeria, the
Kingdom of Benin was one of the oldest and most highly
developed states in West Africa. European visitors were
amazed at the size of Great Benin and the architecture
of its buildings. It would remain a major power in West
Africa until the nineteenth century.

Black Loyalists were the descendants of scholars, traders and artisans as well as farmers, hunters and fishers.

Their ancestors built walled cities, engaged in commerce
and diplomacy with European explorers and created
music, literature and fine art. But when they were forced
from their homeland and compelled to adopt Eurocentric
ways, values and languages, they lost their African heritage. Once they reclaimed their freedom hundreds of
years later, it fell to them to integrate what they could
reclaim with a new history, new traditions and a new
place in the world.

Slavery in America before the Revolution

(1619 – 1775)

Slavery has been part of the human condition since Biblical times. In Africa, prisoners of war, debtors and criminals became enslaved to others, but they were not considered "property." The slavery that Europeans introduced to the New World was precedent-setting for its cruel treatment, its barbarous racism and its callous disregard for life. The enslavement of Africans by Europeans began in the 1440s with the Portuguese, but it soon became a source of riches for the Spanish, French, Dutch and English. By the eighteenth century, the British and their American colonists dominated the slave trade.

This photo shows a display board with a number of details of Black Loyalist history. The man with the scarred back depicts the cruelty of slavery.

Slave traders lead a caravan of kidnapped Africans to the coast for deportation to plantations in the New World. These people were captured along the western coast of Africa.

This detail of the story quilt shows the experiences of enslaved Africans in Britain's North American colonies from Georgia in the south to Nova Scotia in the northeast.

For example, Bunce Island, on the Sierra Leone River in West Africa, was a major holding "factory" where Africans were kept chained, sometimes for months, until they were forced onto ships heading for the New World. It was the last that tens of thousands of them — including those who would become Black Loyalists — ever saw of their continent.

Over the course of four hundred years, 12.5 million Africans were forced into slavery. Most would be put to work on sugar plantations in the West Indies and Latin America. Five per cent were sold to colonists in North America where, in addition to domestic service, they were ordered to harvest crops of tobacco, rice and indigo. Children born into slavery also worked, completing housework, feeding animals and looking after younger children. They were considered ready for full-time work by the age of ten.

The European empires that colonized the New World had regarded Africans as a readily exploitable source of labour since 1619 when English traders first brought Africans to Virginia to work on tobacco plantations. The concept of enslaving people for their entire lives became accepted practice twenty-one years later. In 1641, Massachusetts became the first British colony to legalize the enslaving of Africans.

The practice was not restricted to English colonies. In 1628, an African boy was recorded as New France's first known slave. By 1709, King Louis XIV gave his North American colonists the right to own slaves.

Twenty-one years later, Great Britain had become the world's largest slave-trading country, delivering Africans to colonies that required unpaid labourers to work at the backbreaking tasks of raising rice, tobacco and sugar. By 1750, slavery was legal and practised in all of Britain's North American colonies, including Nova Scotia. (In the 1760s, New England Planters brought an estimated 150 slaves with them to the colony. One naval officer who bought land near Halifax owned sixteen slaves.)

Only the Quakers of Pennsylvania actively forbade their fellow congregants from owning slaves. Their influence did little to stop the transatlantic importation of over 5,000 Africans to America each year.

CHARLESTOWN, *April* 27, 1769.

TO BE SOLD,

On WEDNESDAY *the* Tenth Day *of* MAY *next,*

A CHOICE CARGO OF

Two Hundred & Fifty

NEGROES:

ARRIVED in the Ship COUNTESS of SUSSEX, THOMAS DAVIES, Mafter, directly from GAMBIA, by

JOHN CHAPMAN, & Co.

*** THIS *is the Veffel that had the Small-Pox on Board at the Time of her Arrival the* 31ft *of March laft: Every neceffary Precaution hath fince been taken to cleanfe both Ship and Cargo thoroughly,*

An advertisement from a colonial newspaper announcing the sale of recently arrived African captives. Note the way in which the ad underscores the point that the slaves had not been exposed to smallpox, a perennial concern in the eighteenth century. During the American Revolution, there were more deaths due to smallpox than due to bloodshed on the battlefield.

By 1775, slavery had become so widespread throughout Britain's North American empire that one in five non-Indigenous Americans was a person of African descent. Despite slave uprisings and revolts over two centuries, as well as petitions for their freedom, Africans were unable to achieve emancipation on their own. Only the few that could earn enough money to buy their freedom — or who were emancipated in their masters' wills — had any chance of attaining the legal status of free men and women in North American society.

In the end, it was Britain's pragmatic need for more troops, rather than a desire to abolish slavery in America, that provided a means for some enslaved Africans to become free men and women.

On November 7, 1775, Lord Dunmore, the last royal governor of Virginia, issued a declaration stating that any slaves who joined the British war effort would be granted their freedom. Thanks to the empire's need for more loyal supporters, the Black men and women of the Thirteen Colonies now had the means to actively seek and obtain their own freedom. And as many as 9,000 seized that opportunity.

I Am an Eyewitness

Transcribed here is an interview excerpt with Warwick Francis (1812), a Black Loyalist who settled in New Brunswick in September 1783. Five years earlier he had been enslaved by Dr. Aaron Jellot of Charleston, South Carolina. Years later he shared what he had seen as a slave.

I have also seen Joseph Belseford in the same County chain two of his slaves and make them walk on a plank at a mill pond and those 2 got drowned and they said Joseph Belseford gave a man 360 lashes and then washed him down with salt and water and after that took brand that he branded his Cattle with and make the brand red hot and put it on his buttocks the same as you would brand a creature.

I have seen John Crimshire, overseer on Barnard Elliott's estate, {give punishment to} a man whose name is Tom. {He} had 300 lashes and {was} put on the picket with his left hand tied to his left toe behind him and his right hand to a post and his right foot on the pickets till it worked through his foot {evidently a form of torture involving an iron picket fence}.

John Drayton I have seen him take his slave and put them in a {barrel} and nailed spikes in the {barrel} and roll down a steep hill. The cruelty and punishment of the slave which I have seen would not permit me to make mention but for lashes 300 or 400 and to be washed down with salt and water is but slight punishment.

Many poor {pregnant} women which I have seen likely to be deliver the child and oblige to a mouth piece {to prevent them from stealing food and eating it} and lock out the back part of it, the keys the driver keeps and are obliged to work all day and at night put in the close houses {confinement cells}. I have seen them with a thumbscrew screwed until the blood gushed out of their nails. This I have seen at Isaac MacPherson's . . . this is what I have said I am an eyewitness to it; it is not what I have heard.

Liberty and the American Revolution

(1775 – 1783)

J.S. Copley's painting shows a Black combatant fighting side by side with British forces against American patriots. While not illustrating either the contributions of the Black Brigade or the Black Pioneers — two Black Loyalist corps — it is an 18th century illustration that recognizes the military contributions of free Blacks during the American Revolution.

When considering the history of Black Loyalists, it is important to point out a distinction in the use of the word "Loyalist." While white Americans were considered to have been loyal to the crown for bearing arms, losing property to Patriots, defending British interests in their published works or simply having Loyalist political convictions, a Black man or woman was only considered a Loyalist (and therefore a free person) if he or she served in the war effort for at least a year after coming within the British lines. Black Loyalists *earned* their liberty by *service*, not through mere principles or oaths of allegiance. Fortunately, the stories of how Black Loyalists won their freedom have not been lost.

Titus Cornelius, a Black Loyalist, gained fame as "Colonel Tye." One of the original members of Lord

Dunmore's Ethiopian Regiment, Tye eventually commanded as many as eight hundred white and Black Loyalists in raids on military outposts, plantations and individual rebel homes in southern New Jersey. His Black Brigade was among the last Loyalist military units to evacuate New York City in November 1783.

Other Black Loyalists served with British regiments in non-combat roles. The *Book of Negroes* ledger notes the services of eight trumpeters in the King's American Dragoons and four drummers in the German Knoblach regiment.

Free men also worked within the British forces as "pioneers." In the military jargon of the eighteenth century, a pioneer was a soldier who cleared land, dug latrines and performed other engineering duties. Formed in 1776, the Black Pioneers were the largest African military unit to serve during the American Revolution, making important contributions to the British war effort. For many Africans, enlisting in this unit was their ticket to freedom. No doubt many would gladly have borne arms in the British army, but they were denied admission to both the regular army and white Loyalist regiments.

However, the German troops that the British government hired to supplement their army had no qualms about arming Black soldiers. The Hessen-Kassel and Hessen-Hanau regiments had 115 Africans on their muster lists. The Erbprinz Regiment had enlisted Black Loyalist soldiers as early as 1777, and then added to those

numbers before going to Virginia in 1781. Africans were among the German dead at the Battle of Yorktown. By 1783, as many as eighty-three free Africans had served as drummers for Hessian troops. Black Loyalists also served the British Army as spies and wagon drivers.

The manifest for one of the evacuation vessels that brought Black Loyalists to Nova Scotia reveals the many skills that these allies of the British Crown employed during the American Revolution. On board the *Danger* were those who had served as carpenters, labourers, artificers, collar makers, wheelers and servants in the Royal Artillery. Others found work with the Quartermaster General's Department, the Commissary and the Forage and Provision Department.

From 1775 to 1783, Black Loyalists had been faithful in fulfilling their duties to the British Crown, serving the empire in exchange for their emancipation. It had been a foregone conclusion that Britain — one of the greatest European powers — would speedily quash the Americans. Consequently, Black Loyalists were devastated when they learned that the Patriots had won the war. With the defeat of the British army, they wondered what would become of them, and feared they would be forced to return to enslavement.

A Black Loyalist Spy

In 1782, the British command sent a Black Loyalist known only as Harry on a reconnaissance mission from Monck's Corner, South Carolina. Patriots captured him and — having declared him a British spy — had him executed without benefit of a trial. The racism of the time is evident in the fact that instead of the usual death by hanging meted out to white Loyalists, Harry was beheaded. Furthermore, his head was put on a stake where it could be seen when the British forces marched by. Although Harry received no posthumous medals or awards, his death was noted in military correspondence with the British government on November 27, 1782.

The Loyalist Losers of 1783

EMANCIPATED OR ENSLAVED?

NEW-YORK, 21ᵗʰ *April* 1783.

THIS is to certify to whomſoever it may concern, that the Bearer hereof *Cato Ramſay* a Negro, reſorted to the Britiſh Lines, in conſequence of the Proclamations of Sir William Howe, and Sir Henry Clinton, late Commanders in Chief in America ; and that the ſaid Negro has hereby his Excellency Sir Guy Carleton's Permiſſion to go to Nova-Scotia, or wherever elſe *He* may think proper.

By Order of Brigadier General Birch,

An example of the document which the British used to emancipate a Black Loyalists. Having promised the former slaves of Patriots their freedom if they joined the British cause, the crown — through Sir Guy Carleton — officially recognized the new status of the Black Loyalists by means of this certificate. Since the commandant of New York City, Brigadier General Samuel Birch, signed most of these certificates, they became known as General Birch Certificates (GBC).

The Black Loyalists had pinned all of their hopes for emancipation on a British victory over the Patriot and French forces. When General Cornwallis surrendered to the rebel army and its allies at Yorktown, Virginia, on October 19, 1781, re-enslavement of Britain's Black allies seemed a foregone conclusion.

Over the next two years, as a peace treaty was being negotiated in Paris, Black Loyalists and their white counterparts streamed out of the rebel colonies, seeking sanctuary in New York City and elsewhere in territory still controlled by the British. The first Loyalist evacuation fleet that left Savannah, Georgia, in July of 1782 carried an unrecorded number of Black Loyalists to sanctuary.

Ships bearing both white and Black refugees left Charleston, South Carolina, in December of that year. They took their passengers south to Jamaica and north to Halifax, Nova Scotia. Among the 5,327 Black Loyalists aboard these vessels were one hundred families who would help to found Preston Township, the first settlement of emancipated slaves in British North America. These South Carolina refugees settled outside of Dartmouth, across the harbour from Halifax.

If the victorious Americans had had their way, Black Loyalists who fled Savannah and Charleston in 1782 would have been the only Africans to have secured their freedom in the wake of the Revolution. The treaty negotiations in Paris, France, had begun on November 30 with the signing of the preliminary draft for a peace treaty. It included an article that forbade the British from "carrying away any Negroes or other property of American inhabitants." Given the importance of bringing about a speedy end to the war, it looked as if the British would renege on their promise to grant freedom to their Black Loyalist allies.

Following the Loyalist evacuations of Savannah and Charleston, New York City — the headquarters for the British command throughout the Revolution — became a magnet for loyal Americans desperate to flee persecution, imprisonment and the seizure of their worldly goods. Surrounded by a new nation that wanted to return Black

Loyalists to slavery, New York City was the last sanctuary for Britain's Black allies.

Fortunately, Sir Guy Carleton, the British commander in chief in New York, refused to regard Black Loyalists as property — or as allies that could be abandoned at the end of the Revolution. The British Crown had promised them their freedom, and — despite vigorous opposition from the new United States government — Carleton was determined to treat them as free citizens of the empire. He considered every Black man and woman who had sided with Britain by

An illustration of New York City and Staten Island. Both were under the control of the British throughout the American Revolution. They were sanctuaries for Loyalist refugees, both Black and white. New York City was the departure point for most Black Loyalists fleeing the new United States of America throughout 1783.

December 31, 1782, to be emancipated and therefore no longer the "property of American inhabitants." His interpretation of their status frustrated the intent of the peace treaty's negotiators to return the ex-slaves to their American owners.

To placate American fears that Patriot slaves had been part of the Loyalist evacuation, Carleton commissioned the creation of a ledger to list the names, circumstances and former masters of every Black who left New York City by ship in 1783. This ledger would become known as the *Book of Negroes*.

Up until this point, the liberty that the British had granted Black Loyalists was not much more than a verbal "gentleman's agreement." In an age that valued legal documentation, signatures and seals of authority, there was nothing to legitimize the status of Black Loyalists as free British subjects. Much to the relief of his Black allies, Carleton decided to create a legal document to certify the Black Loyalists' status as free people.

This, as Boston King would later write, "dispelled all our fears, and filled us with joy and gratitude." Armed with their emancipation certificates, Black Loyalists could board the evacuation ships bound for Nova Scotia, Europe, the West Indies and Canada that would take them away from enslavement.

The first fleet of ships to carry Loyalist refugees away from New York under Carleton's command left on April 23, 1783; the last would leave on November 30, 1783. Black passenger numbers ranged from as many as 274 on one vessel to just two on another.

The Black Loyalists had escaped slavery in the American republic; however, they had yet to experience the status they were promised as freed people within the British Empire.

The Founding of Birchtown

(August 1783)

Although Loyalists had begun arriving in Port Roseway on May 5, 1783, it took several months before they were given legal title to plots of land. The settlement had to be surveyed first, a job assigned to Benjamin Marston, a Loyalist from Marblehead, Massachusetts. Newly hired as Nova Scotia's deputy surveyor-general, Marston arrived in Port Roseway at the same time as the first Loyalists. Once they had decided on the site for their new settlement, the refugees began to cut down trees, and Marston started to lay down lines for the settlement's streets.

Lieutenant Lawson, the head of the engineers' department, had been put in charge of overseeing the establishment of Port Roseway by Sir Guy Carleton. In an April 19 letter, he assigned Lawson eleven carpenters, a foreman, a mason and a smith. He also stated that essential to the efforts were a "sergeant, corporal and sixteen of the Black Pioneers." Carleton indicated that all of these skills were needed to create "a town, wharfs, barracks and other public buildings necessary to a great and permanent establishment."

Initially, Port Roseway was to be a new home for both Black and white Loyalists. Within six months' time, a muster showed that the Loyalist settlement had 1,269 free and enslaved Blacks. After the Black Pioneers had cleared the land site and prepared the roads, twenty Black Loyalist families established homes in the refugee settlement.

However, Carleton's vision for Port Roseway did not coincide with that of John Parr, Nova Scotia's governor. Parr instructed that an area known as the northwest arm of the harbour should be made the site of a Black Loyalist community. When, in July, Parr finally visited the Loyalist refugees who had disembarked in Port Roseway, he announced their city would henceforth be known as Shelburne. This may have also been when he charged Marston with surveying the proposed Black settlement.

No records survive to explain why Parr created a separate Black Loyalist settlement. The British had made no contingency plans for the possibility that they might lose the War of Independence, and so they had had no idea how they would fulfill their wartime promises to their Black allies. In the absence of instructions from London, Parr may have simply been making up policy as he went along. If, on the other hand, the decision to form a separate Black settlement was based on white racist attitudes, Black Loyalists did not perceive it as a negative thing. Colonel Stephen Blucke, already recognized as a leader among his people, embraced the opportunity.

On September 3, Blucke and his captains led 500 or more Black Loyalists to the shore of their new settlement. Within a year, their numbers would swell to over 1,530 people, making the town the largest free Black settlement outside of Africa.

Marston's diary contains the first known reference to the name "Birchtown." On Sunday, September 7, 1783, the surveyor wrote that he had sent his assistants to "Birch-Town today out for the Blacks." But the long delay in finally assigning land to the Black settlers meant that there was no time to plant crops before the winter. The only source of income for the men would be as labourers in the construction of houses for Shelburne's white Loyalists.

Not every white Loyalist family had a finished house for its first winter in Nova Scotia. Canvas tents, cellars and log huts were the only shelters available for those who came in the fall of 1783.

While those Black Loyalists who had arrived earlier in the year had time to build huts with doors or make do with army tents, some of Birchtown's first residents were forced to draw upon their experiences in the Black Pioneers. Having been responsible for building temporary shelters for the British Army, they used those rudimentary structures as their models, and built pit houses to see them through the winter.

This watercolour shows an unnamed Black Loyalist at work as a sawyer (wood-cutter) in Shelburne in 1788. This was just one of the many trades that Black craftsmen brought to Nova Scotia.

Birchtown

The Black Loyalists named their settlement in honour of Brigadier General Samuel Birch who signed their emancipation papers, thus making them free men and women.

This photo shows the cramped quarters within a pit house. Somehow, dozens of families survived the Nova Scotia winter in spaces like this that were just over one cubic metre in size.

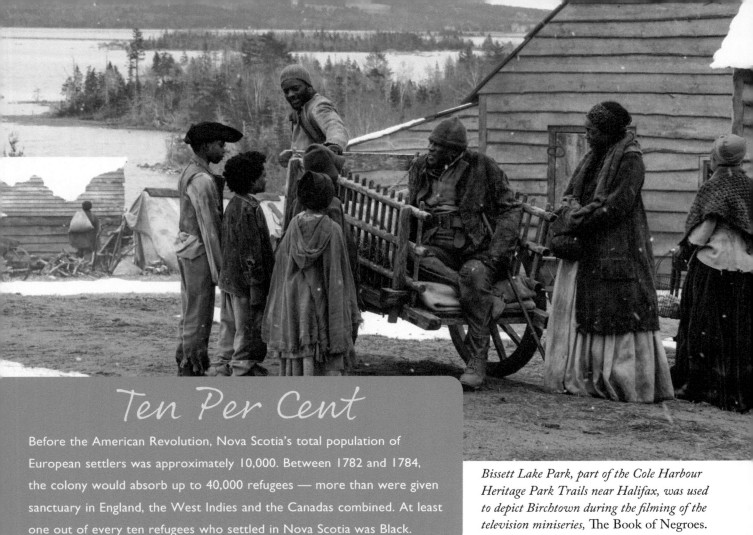

Ten Per Cent

Before the American Revolution, Nova Scotia's total population of European settlers was approximately 10,000. Between 1782 and 1784, the colony would absorb up to 40,000 refugees — more than were given sanctuary in England, the West Indies and the Canadas combined. At least one out of every ten refugees who settled in Nova Scotia was Black.

Bissett Lake Park, part of the Cole Harbour Heritage Park Trails near Halifax, was used to depict Birchtown during the filming of the television miniseries, The Book of Negroes.

Winter came early in 1783. Snow would soon cover the terrain that in the spring would prove to be so difficult to farm. The nearby forest was home to moose and deer; the bay had plenty of fish. Contact with the local Mi'kmaw people was no doubt a great help to the newly freed settlers, providing them with the skills needed to survive their first winter.

Despite these hardships, the people of Birchtown faced their future with faith and determination. This same tenacity characterized Black Loyalist settlers wherever they put down roots throughout the Maritime Provinces.

The next eight years would test that resolve again and again as free and enslaved Blacks across the region struggled with government neglect and outright racism not only from those in power, but from a community and province that did not accept them. But it was also a time that saw the establishment of schools and churches, the building blocks of strong community life. These extraordinary times demanded ordinary people to step forward as their communities' leaders. Fortunately, the Black Loyalists had no shortage of heroes.

Seeking Land, Seeking Justice
(1783 – 1791)

The story of the Black Loyalists is told through a quilt that is displayed at the Black Loyalist Heritage Centre. This panel illustrates the early years of settlement in Nova Scotia.

While Birchtown's pioneers readied themselves for a North Atlantic winter, the Black Loyalist who would leave an indelible mark on all of their lives was impatiently waiting for spring to arrive so that he could continue his interrupted journey to Nova Scotia.

Born free among the Egba people of Nigeria, Thomas Peters was kidnapped by slavers when he was twenty-two years old. A French colonist in Louisiana purchased Peters and later sold him to an American in North Carolina. Following his escape from his enslaver when he was thirty-eight years old, Peters became a sergeant in the Black Pioneers. This company was among the last group of free Blacks to leave New York City in the fall of 1783. Boarding the *Joseph* on November 9, the Black Pioneers thought that they would be disembarking at Annapolis Royal, Nova Scotia, within a matter of weeks. However, a hurricane drove their ship off course, forcing its captain to find shelter in Bermuda, where it remained until the spring.

In April of 1784, the *Joseph* finally sailed into the Annapolis Basin. There, the leadership skills that Peters had acquired during his years of command in the Black Pioneers came to the fore. The Black Loyalist oversaw the establishment of Brindley Town, the second largest free Black settlement in Nova Scotia. It was initially settled by seventy-six Black Loyalist families — two hundred people. This community was near Digby, a Loyalist town at the mouth of the Annapolis Basin.

Sir Guy Carleton respected the Black Pioneers and had high expectations for their success. In the fall of 1783, Carleton wrote a Nova Scotian official, "I recommend them to your protection and beg you will apply to Governor Parr, that in case they settle near any of the towns they may have a town lot as at Shelburne." It fell to Thomas Peters to make Carleton's hopes a reality.

Most of the Africans who had settled in the Digby area were veterans of the Black Pioneers, so Peters was someone they knew and trusted — a man who could deal with land and provision problems that had been festering since the Black Loyalists had arrived. While white Loyalists received three years of provisions from the government, Black Loyalists had received only eighty days' worth. In order to receive those provisions, Black Loyalists had to work at building roads, a condition never placed on the white Loyalists.

Within two months of his arrival, Peters and a fellow Black Pioneer, Murphy Steele, petitioned the Nova Scotia government, asking for land grants equal to what white Loyalists had received. It responded by surveying one-acre *town* lots in Brindley Town, but there was great confusion over *farming* lots. Black Loyalists had to be relocated twice because of disputes over who had the right to settle on particular lots. In the meantime, the free Blacks fed themselves by fishing in the nearby Bay of Fundy and growing vegetables in small gardens.

Some white Loyalists and British charities rallied to their cause, establishing a school by January of 1785. Methodist and Anglican churches sprang up within the Black Loyalist settlement. The infrastructure of community life was slowly beginning to form, but without means to sustain themselves, Black Loyalists would be forced to abandon their settlement.

Frustrated by the government's slow response to his petition, Peters decided to leave Brindley Town in July of 1785. Accompanied by other Black Pioneer veterans, he crossed the Bay of Fundy to the recently created colony of New Brunswick. In October, he petitioned Thomas Carleton, the lieutenant governor of New Brunswick, for farm land on the St. John River. Peters also represented fifteen Black Loyalist families who wanted a school built for their children.

However, the former Black Pioneer's quest for equal rights was no more successful in New Brunswick than it had been in Brindley Town. Angered by the lack of action on the part of colonial governments, Peters prepared a petition that he would personally deliver to the British cabinet. Given power of attorney by over two hundred families in Nova Scotia and New Brunswick, Peters set sail for Great Britain in the fall of 1790 to seek justice for his fellow Black Loyalists.

Peters was not the first Black Loyalist to seek fair treatment in New Brunswick. Created by the separation of Nova Scotia's land mass into two provinces in 1784, New Brunswick was the first colony in the British empire to be founded by refugees. Its motto "Hope Restored" captured the optimism of its white founders, but for its Black Loyalist settlers their experience in the colony was "Hope Delayed."

Richard Wheeler Corankapone was one of the 243 Black Loyalists who arrived at the mouth of the St. John River aboard the *Clinton* in August of 1783.

Unfortunately, the racist attitudes of the late eighteenth century accompanied the British officials and loyal refugees who had settled in New Brunswick. When the city of St. John was incorporated in 1785, Black Loyalists were denied the right to any occupation within the city other than as menial labourers or servants. They could not fish in the harbour or have a trade. St. John's charter declared that "American and European white inhabitants" could be free citizens of the city and enjoy "all the liberties, privileges and pre-eminences of freemen." However, "people of colour or black people . . . are . . . excluded the privilege of being or becoming free citizens."

Black Loyalists could not become merchants, tavern keepers, tanners, carpenters, bakers or blacksmiths as white "freemen" could. The very skills that made Black Loyalists such valued allies of the British during the American Revolution could not be exercised in a settlement that proudly called itself the Loyalist City.

Thus in 1785, thirty-four Black Loyalists, including fifteen of his shipmates, asked Corankapone to be their "captain" and petition the government for land outside the city. Corankapone reminded New Brunswick's lieutenant governor that "the Blacks in general have been thought Loyal and have throughout the Rebellion been generally ready to obey any Orders from the British Commander." He pointed out that the Blacks wanted to "lead Industrious, honest Lives and instead of Being a Burden, should be an Advantage to the Community . . . Your Excellency's Petitioner therefore most humbly Prays a Grant may be made to the Blacks named in the annexed List of the Land . . . or such Relief in their Wretched Circumstances."

The Black Loyalists did not receive their grants until 1787. How they survived in the intervening years is unrecorded. Many died. For some, becoming the indentured servants of white Loyalists seemed like the only way that they could provide for themselves or their children.

Land

When Black Loyalists arrived in the Atlantic colonies, it is believed that the British intended for them to receive the same amount of land as all other disbanded soldiers. The normal arrangements would either be a small town lot and fifty acres of farmland, or a two hundred acre farm in less settled country. That is an accurate summary of what most white Loyalists received; the average farm grant was close to seventy-five acres. In Shelburne, some whites had to wait for as long as three years to receive their land. The Black Loyalists, on the other hand, were not so fortunate. While some eventually received town lots — less than what was promised — the majority received no farmland at all. Those lots that were granted were on poor soil, small, remote and very late in coming. In Birchtown, only 184 of the 649 male settlers received land, after waiting five years to receive grants that were less than half the average for whites.

Without land to produce crops to feed themselves or sell in Shelburne, some Black Loyalists' only hope for survival was to hire out their labour in a sharecropping arrangement or to indenture themselves to Shelburne's settlers. The latter, if they were men of integrity, would provide food, clothing, shelter and training in a trade during the period of indenture. Sadly, for many Black Loyalists, indentureships were little more than a return to slavery.

The Attack on the Black Loyalists

(1784)

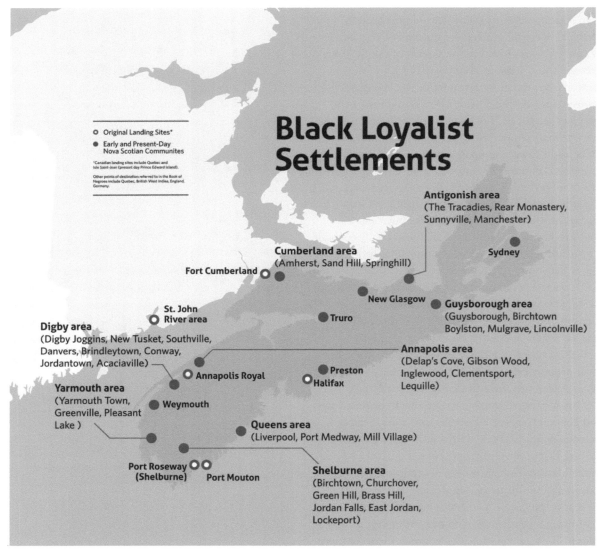

Black Loyalist Settlements

○ Original Landing Sites*
● Early and Present-Day Nova Scotian Communites

*Canadian landing sites include Quebec and Isle Saint-Jean (present day Prince Edward Island).

Other points of destination referred to in the Book of Negroes include Quebec, British West Indies, England, Germany.

Antigonish area
(The Tracadies, Rear Monastery, Sunnyville, Manchester)

Sydney

Cumberland area
(Amherst, Sand Hill, Springhill)

Fort Cumberland ○

New Glasgow

Guysborough area
(Guysborough, Birchtown Boylston, Mulgrave, Lincolnville)

St. John River area ○

Truro

Digby area
(Digby Joggins, New Tusket, Southville, Danvers, Brindleytown, Conway, Jordantown, Acaciaville)

Annapolis area
(Delap's Cove, Gibson Wood, Inglewood, Clementsport, Lequille)

○ Annapolis Royal

Preston

Halifax ○

Yarmouth area
(Yarmouth Town, Greenville, Pleasant Lake)

Weymouth

Queens area
(Liverpool, Port Medway, Mill Village)

Port Roseway ○ ○
(Shelburne) Port Mouton

Shelburne area
(Birchtown, Churchover, Green Hill, Brass Hill, Jordan Falls, East Jordan, Lockeport)

This map shows both the original settlements of the Black Loyalists in Nova Scotia as well as areas they settled in the years following 1783. The settlements along the Atlantic coast from Halifax to Annapolis Royal heard of the opportunity to migrate to Sierra Leone. The remaining settlements did not.

While Black Loyalists were building a variety of shelters to see themselves through their first winter in Birchtown, David George continued to preach to both Black and White believers in nearby Shelburne. The pastor of the first all-Black Baptist Church in North America, George escaped slavery in South Carolina at thirty-six years old, and joined the British in 1779. He and his family sailed with other Loyalists who fled Charleston for sanctuary in Halifax, Nova Scotia, in the fall of 1782.

Hearing of a significant Black population in Shelburne, George journeyed there in June 1783. An ardent evangelist, George baptized new believers and by Christmas 1783 established the first Baptist congregation in the Maritimes entirely comprised of Loyalist refugees. While the Baptist preacher's interracial ministry raised the ire of many in Shelburne, he was sought out as a preacher by Protestant sects in nearby communities.

The trials of their first year in Shelburne had made the city's white Loyalists frustrated and bitter. The land that they had expected to receive had not been surveyed or allocated. The promises of a prosperous port city that would draw on a rich fishery and fertile farming communities were impossible to fulfill. As so often happened in a time of discontent within a white community, its resident Black citizens bore the brunt of its anger.

Over the past year, Black Loyalists of Shelburne and Birchtown had willingly worked for the lower wages offered them by the more prosperous white settlers, building houses and roads for the new settlement. Shelburne's disbanded Loyalist soldiers, who were also in need of gainful employment, refused to accept the same wages as Blacks.

With no land and no jobs, the ever-mounting frustration of the veterans only needed a spark to erupt into violence. David George, the local Baptist minister, had begun publicly immersing white converts. Their baptisms signaled the fact that they had united with his predominantly Black congregation. What *could* have been the beginning of a society in which Blacks and whites could worship together became, instead, the spark that ignited days of race riots.

On July 26, 1784, the frustrated ex-servicemen erupted into a mob — some arming themselves with muskets, others using the pulleys, iron hooks and ropes from nearby ships as weapons. After demolishing George's house, they destroyed almost two dozen Black homes situated near the minister's property. The soldiers beat George, driving him into a nearby swamp. In the wake of these attacks, hundreds of Shelburne's Black Loyalists fled to the safety of nearby Birchtown.

The rioting did not stop with the destruction of Shelburne's Black community. The mob attacked anyone they saw of African descent, whether they were sole travellers or those fleeing from the riots. None of the whites that had employed Black Loyalists responded to the Blacks' screams of terror or to the destruction of their workers' homes. The reign of terror against the Black community lasted ten days, but the racial attacks continued for a full month. Finally, troops arrived from Halifax in an effort to restore order. When the rule of law was re-established, the government's only real action was to placate the white Loyalists. There was no offer of aid or assistance to the persecuted Black people and no efforts made to provide restitution for their lost property and belongings. Black Loyalists were free in Nova Scotia, but certainly not equal. This official response to white violence directed at Black Loyalists clearly demonstrated that. The riots and their aftermath simply shed light on what had already been there.

While the Shelburne race riots were started by a small mob, the fact its numbers grew and remained unchecked by the rest of the community further unmasked the racist attitudes of Shelburne's 12,000 citizens. All it took for evil men to succeed was for good men to do nothing. And those who considered themselves to be the virtuous Loyalists of Shelburne did nothing to stop the violence. They were complicit in the bloodshed.

After reclaiming his meeting house — which had been used as a tavern in his absence — David George began to minister to other Blacks who had ventured back to Shelburne. Neither white Loyalists' persecution of the previous year, nor the banning of "Negro frolics" had dampened George's evangelistic zeal. That summer his perseverance in preaching the gospel was rewarded by a "considerable revival of religion."

Over the next seven years, George's reputation as a preacher grew. Blacks in both Nova Scotia and New Brunswick invited him to visit. The Baptist leader appointed elders over the congregations that he founded and kept in contact with these Black faith communities. In the process of building up his denomination, George was helping to empower and affirm community leaders and was establishing vital communication links between the new Black Loyalist settlements of the Maritimes.

Other Black Loyalist ministers such as John Marrant and Boston King were also building communities through their work with Methodist congregations. If these three pastors had all died before the summer of 1791, their roles in shaping Black Loyalist society would still have been noteworthy.

Along with the growth of Black Loyalist churches in Nova Scotia and New Brunswick, the years following the establishment of Birchtown were also witness to the growth of schools. These would also play an important part in creating a new society, empowering educated Black men and women to equip the next generation for life in the Maritimes.

The years between 1785 and 1791 witnessed the establishment of schools in five Black Loyalist communities. Their teachers, all veterans of the American Revolution, were Thomas Brownspriggs, Joseph Leonard, William Furmage, Mrs. Catherine Abernathy and Col. Stephen Blucke.

The Second Exodus to Freedom
(1792)

This portrait of Thomas Peters was painted during his 1791 visit to the UK. It is the only likeness of a Black Loyalist known to exist. Peters returned to the Maritimes with news of the opportunity to found a colony of free Blacks in Sierra Leone in West Africa. He is one of the crucial figures in Black Loyalist history.

During his time in Black settlements on both sides of the Bay of Fundy, Thomas Peters had come to be acknowledged as the "one person nominated and appointed to act for and on behalf" of the colony's Black Loyalists "in all matters both civil and religious." Neither a preacher nor a teacher, Peters's leadership skills were refined during his military service with the Black Pioneers.

Since his arrival in Nova Scotia in 1784, Peters authored petitions demanding equal treatment for his people. Despite the promises made to them during the American Revolution, less than half of the Black Loyalists had any land at all, let alone the guaranteed hundred acres. Landless and hungry, many free blacks had effectively lost their liberty. Peters knew of men "reduced to slavery," forced into indenture contracts, while others had been seized and made slaves once more.

Frustrated with the lack of action in Nova Scotia and New Brunswick, Peters went to the heart of the empire to seek justice in the fall of 1790. While in London, he met with the leading abolitionists of the day: Granville Sharp, William Wilberforce and Thomas Clarkson, the founders of the British Anti-Slavery Society. *Finally*, his complaints received the hearing they deserved.

A portrait of John Clarkson, the Englishman who represented the Sierra Leone Company and recruited the Black Loyalists of Nova Scotia and New Brunswick for a new colony in West Africa. He was the brother of the famous abolitionist Thomas Clarkson. John Clarkson accompanied the Black Loyalists on their journey from Halifax, Nova Scotia to Freetown, Sierra Leone in 1792.

By August 6, 1790, the British Secretary for the Colonies wrote to the governors of Nova Scotia and New Brunswick with copies of Peters's list of grievances, agreeing with the Black Loyalist that his people "have certainly strong grounds for complaint." It was unprecedented — the imperial government had ordered two colonial governors to give serious regard to the injustices and unequal treatment endured by free Blacks.

In his letter, the colonial secretary also suggested two alternatives for Black Loyalists who, because of their ill treatment, might no longer wish to stay in New Brunswick and Nova Scotia. They had the option of going to the West Indies and serving in free Black regiments *or* they could receive free passage to Sierra Leone and settle there. The gamble that Thomas Peters had taken in bringing his complaints directly to the British government had paid off. He returned to the Maritimes in August to spread the news of his triumph.

Given the way in which Black Loyalist concerns had been ignored and belittled in the past, the Sierra Leone Company also felt that it would be wise to send one of their own members to Nova Scotia to oversee the exodus to West Africa. Twenty-seven-year-old John Clarkson took on the task, arriving in Halifax on October 7, 1791. John was the brother of Thomas Clarkson who, with William Wilberforce and Granville Sharp, helped to found the Committee for the Abolition of the African Slave Trade in 1787.

Clarkson eventually visited Shelburne, where he was greeted by minister David George and later spoke to a large gathering of interested Black Loyalists. When Clarkson spoke to Black Loyalists in Birchtown, almost 400 people packed into the Methodist meeting house. Many shared the conviction held by one older man who confided to the British abolitionist, "If one die, had rather me die in my own country than in this cold place."

Opposition to the Sierra Leone project came from members of the white Loyalist community who had come to depend upon cheap Black labour. They spread false rumours about what would happen to those who immigrated to West Africa. White employers withheld Blacks' wages, put false debts in account books, slandered men's good character, offered bribes and even threatened violence, all in an effort to prevent the loss of inexpensive labourers and valued consumers for local produce.

Clarkson realized that Blacks were "considered in this province in no better light than beasts." Recognizing the degree of antagonism to the project, David George confided to Clarkson that if certain parties knew that the two of them had been meeting, "my life would not be safe."

The situation was no better in New Brunswick. The cruelest ploy was to demand that Black Loyalists must produce their "free pass" (General Birch certificates) if

The Black Loyalist Heritage Centre quilt tells the story of the Nova Scotians' arrival in Sierra Leone (the Lion Mountains) on Africa's west coast.

they wanted to leave the colony. These pieces of paper had been given to them in 1783 to certify that the British government had set them free, and most had been lost, destroyed or damaged over the intervening eight years. Other officials forged indenture certificates and loan documents made out in the names of the Black Loyalists who were anxious to leave for Sierra Leone, in an attempt to keep them in New Brunswick.

Heeding George's warnings of possible violent opposition in other communities, Clarkson decided not to visit Digby and Annapolis Royal, and returned to Halifax following his recruiting mission to Shelburne County. Neither Clarkson nor any other champion of the Sierra Leone project visited the Black Loyalist settlements in Guysborough County, Cape Breton or Antigonish County. Consequently, they would become the only settlements unshaken by the exodus to Africa, an exodus that would diminish or completely deplete Black Loyalist communities in other parts of the Maritimes.

After months of preparation, the four ships, nine brigs and two schooners that made up the Sierra Leone fleet sailed out of Halifax on Sunday, January 15, 1792. Clarkson wrote that his passengers were "all in good spirits, properly equipped, and — I hope — destined to be happy."

After a long and dangerous journey, nearly 1,200 Black Loyalists arrived in Freetown's harbour on Tuesday, March 6. What they saw as they disembarked gave rise to both hope and despair. They had been led to believe that there would be fortifications overlooking the harbour, that streets would be laid out and that lots would be surveyed and ready for granting. The Black Loyalists came to discover that conditions were very similar to what they met upon their arrival in Port Roseway in 1783: thick forests, no town plan and no scheme to accommodate the newcomers. Rations were in short supply, and during the first few weeks, it rained constantly. Nevertheless, it was a new land of liberty for the Black Loyalists of New Brunswick and Nova Scotia.

Despite these disappointments, when, on March 8, all of the companies' captains met with Clarkson, they expressed "their joy at the safe arrival to a land which . . . seems a most rich and beautiful prospect." The Black Loyalists had neither lost their optimism nor their faith in a better tomorrow.

For the rest of their history in West Africa, the Black Loyalist founders and their descendants would simply be known as "the Nova Scotians." They would help to shape the destiny of a country yet unborn.

Those left behind in Nova Scotia and New Brunswick would share the same task as their friends and relatives in Sierra Leone — playing their part in building a country that in seventy-five years' time would bear the name of Canada.

Sierra Leone Company

The Sierra Leone Company wanted to create an African homeland for free, Christian Blacks. Granville Sharp founded the company in 1788 to provide relief for the Black poor of London. These were Black Loyalist sailors and some slaves who had been freed by the groundbreaking legal decision that ended slavery in England. Their initial settlement, however, failed. Undaunted, Granville Sharp and the Sierra Leone Company continued their efforts. New investors were found, a royal charter was granted, and with the assistance of Thomas Peters the company found a new group of distressed Black Christians to populate their planned colony in West Africa.

The Remnant:
By Choice or By Necessity?
(1792 – 1988)

Rose Fortune came to Nova Scotia in 1783 when she was just nine years old. While other Black Loyalists migrated to Sierra Leone, Rose earned her living as a "trucker" at Annapolis Royal, carrying baggage in a heavy wheelbarrow for the passengers who travelled by ferry between Nova Scotia and New Brunswick. Rose also imposed and enforced curfews at the wharves. Many consider her to be the first female policewoman in what is now Canada.

The year 1792 was a year of loss and recovery. Most of the leadership of the Maritimes' Black Loyalist community had left, as well as a large number of its Baptists and Methodists. Although diminished in number, there were still Blacks living in St. John, New Brunswick, and along the St. John River.

The villages in Nova Scotia's Guysborough and Antigonish Counties remained untouched by the exodus to Sierra Leone. Many of the free Blacks remaining in and around Yarmouth, Annapolis Royal, Horton, Queens County and Preston had chosen not to go to Sierra Leone for their own reasons or because of their status as indentured servants. Less than half of Birchtown's population remained.

One portion of the Maritimes' Black population was completely unaffected by the migration to Sierra Leone. The historian H. A. Whitfield has estimated that at least 2,466 enslaved Blacks came to the Maritimes with the Loyalists (298 in Annapolis, 984 in Shelburne and 1,184 in St. John). These enslaved Blacks would continue to provide free labour to their white masters until the abolition of slavery within the British Empire in 1883. Before that date, Loyalist newspapers regularly carried notices for the sale of slaves; Loyalist wills still bequeathed enslaved Blacks to their heirs.

It would be the task of this faithful remnant of Black Loyalists to survive and thrive in a land of broken promises, bequeathing to their descendants the challenge of making those promises come true.

Today, re-enactor guides, dressed in the attire of the late eighteenth century, share the story of the Black Loyalists with visitors to the Birchtown historic site.

OPPOSITE PAGE: Among the displays in the Black Loyalist Heritage Centre, the names found in the Book of Negroes *ledger have been used to create a man's face.*

Safeguarding Black Loyalist Heritage

(1989 – 2015)

The original building for the Black Loyalist Heritage Society was torched by an arsonist on March 31, 2006. It devastated the community.

Until very recently, the Black Loyalists' story has been left out of the histories of both the American Revolution and the formation of Canada. It became lost in the American narrative of a war that the Patriots fought to overthrow the tyranny of the British king in pursuit of liberty. It was left out of the Canadian narrative of the United Empire Loyalists who founded a nation based on British ideals and the British monarchy. However, in communities scattered across the Maritimes, the descendants of Black Loyalists kept alive the story of sacrifice, service and emancipation, remembering how their ancestors journeyed to a land that promised them equal opportunity.

Over time, organizations such as the Sons of the American Revolution and the United Empire Loyalist Association of Canada emerged within white North American society. They celebrated the heritage of their ancestors — to the point of issuing certificates to verify a person's descent from someone who fought on one side or the other in the War of Independence. It wasn't until 1989 that a society was founded to discover, interpret, safeguard and promote the history and heritage of Black Loyalists.

The 2006 arsonist attack not only destroyed the offices of the BLHS, but also its valuable archives and genealogical data.

What is now known as the Black Loyalist Heritage Society has faced many serious challenges as it worked to fulfill its mandate. Initially known as the Shelburne County Cultural Awareness Society, these Black Loyalist descendants were concerned that the local community was unaware of the contributions made by its ancestors. They began collecting family data and other historical information to raise awareness of Birchtown's significance. "Our hard won successes and strength to reach for the future come from the strength and spirit of our founder and sustaining members."

When a landfill project threatened to destroy much of Birchtown in 1992, the society's role went beyond that of serving as collectors and guardians of genealogical data — they became political activists for the recognition and preservation of Black Loyalist history. Archaeological surveys commissioned in 1993 and 1994 revealed that Birchtown was far from insignificant. Within four years of a petition they prepared, protesting the creation of the landfill, the society had Birchtown recognized as a national historic site. The erection of a monument testifying to the town's significance in 1996 was the beginning of what is now the Black Loyalist heritage site.

Within three years' time, the society had acquired four properties and St. Paul's Church as Canada's first Black Loyalist heritage site and resource centre. In 2000, the Black Loyalist Heritage Society opened a museum in the Birchtown Old Schoolhouse and constructed their office. The society also saw that four members of the local Black community were trained in genealogical research, enabling them to respond to queries from around the world asking for assistance in tracing Black family histories. The society began to compile a Black Loyalist Registry that identified those descended from the original settlers. Since then, over 2,000 self-identified Black Loyalist descendants have become society members.

In 2004, historic re-enactors worked at the heritage site, portraying Black Loyalists who had originally settled in Birchtown. The following year saw the creation of both a map and a website to guide visitors to African Nova

Scotian historic sites as well as the granting of armorial bearings to the Black Loyalist Heritage Society by the Canadian Heraldic Authority.

This ever-growing momentum almost came to a dead stop when, on March 31, 2006, an arsonist's attack gutted the society's Birchtown office building, destroying the genealogical data, historical records and priceless artifacts that had been collected over twenty years. Original photos donated by Black Loyalist descendants were among the items destroyed in the fire. Fortunately, Birchtown's first land grant map was rescued before flames engulfed the building.

Beyond the loss of irreplaceable materials, members of the community lost their sense of safety. Elizabeth Cromwell, the society's president, reacted to the tragedy saying, "I'm assuming they're striking at all of us . . . All I could think of was we're in Nova Scotia. We're not in Alabama."

Eight months later, police finally charged a local man with the destruction of the society's office. Already in jail on a long list of crimes, the suspect was not tried for his arson attack, and so there was never a public airing of the motivation for his crime. Despite the police's refusal to label it as such, Nova Scotia's Black community considered it a hate crime.

Rather than being an ending, the fire became a beginning of new connections and partnerships.

Shelburne's Christ Church donated $10,000 to the rebuilding campaign. Acadia University offered $6,000 and two senior students to restore the society's lost genealogical records. The owners of the Whirligig Bookstore encouraged customers to buy replacement books for the society's burned-out library. The Bank of Nova Scotia launched a national fundraising campaign, stating "The journey of the Black Loyalists to this province is not just part of African Nova Scotian history: it is Nova Scotian heritage and Canadian history. The burning of the office is a tragedy for all." A Halifax-based computer expert volunteered eighty hours to rescue almost all of the data stored on the society's burned computer hard drives.

This renewed momentum continued into 2011 with two special events: the creation of a story quilt (see pp. 61 and 69) and the launch of the Black Loyalist Heritage Fundraising Campaign. As others recognized the importance of the Black Loyalist story, new partners came alongside the society. In 2012, both the federal and provincial governments pledged their support for the Black Loyalist Heritage Centre. They were joined by the Canada Cultural Spaces Fund, the Department of Canadian Heritage and the Atlantic Canada Opportunities Agency. On March 11, 2014, construction of the Black Loyalist Heritage Centre officially began.

By this time, *The Book of Negroes*, Lawrence Hill's 2007 novel about a Black Loyalist woman, had become such an international bestseller that it was being made into a television mini-series. Birchtown was used as one of the film's Nova Scotia locations. Costumes from the series were later donated to the Black Loyalist Heritage Centre.

Momentum continued to build. In 2014, Wanda Taylor's *Birchtown and the Black Loyalists* was published for younger readers. In addition to becoming a resource in Nova Scotia's schools, the Canadian Children's Book Centre listed it as one of the top ten Black history books for youth.

The Black Loyalist Heritage Society has an ongoing commitment to protecting and promoting the African heritage of the Maritime Provinces, so sharing that history with young people of African descent is a high priority. That commitment was one of the motivating factors in the creation of a site to honour Canada's Black founders.

Finally, after years of struggle and setback, the Black Loyalist Heritage Centre officially opened its doors to the public on May 1, 2015, as the twenty-eighth member of the Nova Scotia Museums. The centre now welcomes thousands of visitors from around the world evey year.

As part of its ongoing interpretation program, the BLHS employs historic re-enactors to put a human face on the story of the Black Loyalists. Their clothing gives visitors to the site a sense of the eighteenth century world and illustrates how the Black Loyalists would have appeared had there been cameras in the 1780s.

The Book of Negroes Ledger
BLACK LOYALISTS IN THE FAMILY TREE

A display featuring a computer monitor where visitors to the BLHC can access the data in the 1783 Book of Negroes *ledger. This chapter explains its significance.*

A page from the Book of Negroes *ledger. The columns are entitled "Vessels Names and their Commanders," "Where Bound," "Negros Names," "Age," Description," "Claimants," and "Names of the Persons in whose Possession they now are."*

Commissioned by Sir Guy Carleton, the British commander in chief, the *Book of Negroes* is a 156-page ledger containing the names of more than 3,000 Blacks who left New York City between April and November of 1783. Included among the names of free Black Loyalists are the names of white Loyalists' indentured servants and slaves as well as some Indigenous people. It is important to note that the ledger does not record all of the Blacks who fled the new United States of America to find liberty within the British Empire. Hundreds — perhaps thousands — of unrecorded Black Loyalists left Charleston and Savannah in 1782. Others travelled on merchant vessels and troop ships.

Historians estimate that 4,000 Black Loyalists left New York in 1783. Although only half of that number is recorded in the *Book of Negroes*, the ledger is an important document in piecing together the stories of Black Loyalists.

The *Book of Negroes* ledger was compiled to refute the claims of any American slave owner who might, at a future date, protest that the British had stolen his property as Loyalist refugees fled New York City. Meticulous details on the appearance, age, colony of origin and legal status of departing Africans were recorded in two large ledgers. Should any American in the future make the claim that a particular African had been stolen from him, the ledger could be consulted and the escaped slave could be returned. Happily, there are no accounts of slaves ever being reclaimed by owners who referred to Carleton's ledger in the years following the Revolution.

The information about each person in the ledger was not always uniformly recorded. Some entries for Black Loyalists included references to Birch certificates,

Online Search

Explore the digital *Book of Negroes* online at:
data.novascotia.ca/Arts-Culture-and-History/-
Book-of-Negroes-1783/xxcy-v3fh

degrees of African ancestry or detailed physical descriptions, while others did not. Written by British army personnel, the entries often display the sexist and racist attitudes common in the late eighteenth century. With only seven exceptions, Black women were referred to as "wenches." While none of the men were termed "boys," some were described as being rascals, quadroons, mulattos or mustees.

Officials made two copies of the *Book of Negroes* ledger; one was stored in the United States and one kept in archives in Britain. It wasn't until the latter half of the twentieth century that Canadian scholars were able to access the ledger's data through microfilmed copies. For the first time, if one knew the ship upon which a slave or Black Loyalist had departed New York City, the names of its African passengers could be discovered. Since its rediscovery, this ledger has become a key source for piecing together the story of the founders of Canada's African heritage.

The *Book of Negroes* ledger is also an excellent starting point for the keen genealogist or period historian. With the name of a particular Black Loyalist at hand, a family researcher can then seek out other documents from the American Revolution that can be found online. Is the person mentioned in the correspondence of Sir Guy Carleton? In petitions to colonial governments? In John Clarkson's journal? Does he/she appear in subsequent muster rolls in Shelburne or Digby? In transcripts of the newspapers of early New York City, New Brunswick and Nova Scotia? In colonial probate records? In the victualling lists for St. John's Fort Howe?

Stout

— a term used to denote good health and strength rather than obesity. It was used of both whites and blacks in the eighteenth century, but is especially common in the *Book of Negroes*.

Taken from inside the exhibition hall, this shot focuses on names from the Book of Negroes, *a primary source of Black Loyalist history. The outdoors can be seen through the glass.*

A close-up of a page from the Book of Negroes. *This ledger was commissioned by Sir Guy Carleton, the British commander in chief stationed in New York City, to record the names and circumstances of all free and enslaved Blacks leaving the United States with the loyalist evacuation fleets. Created to allay the fears of American slave owners who hoped to reclaim their freed slaves, the ledger has become an invaluable source of data on the Black Loyalists.*

Wench

— the racist and derogatory word used for 829 of the black females listed in the *Book of Negroes*. Only nine were described as "women" in the ledger; four were called "negresses". "Wench" had meanings ranging from "lower class woman" to "female servant" to "prostitute".

21st century connections

Thanks to the genealogy television series, *Who Do You Think You Are?*, one of Canada's leading opera stars was able to trace her roots back to a Black Loyalist couple listed in the *Book of Negroes*. Measha Brueggergosman, a native of Fredericton, New Brunswick, discovered that her great-great-great-great-grandparents were part of the Loyalist evacuation to Nova Scotia. According to data recorded in Carleton's ledger, John Gosman and his wife Rose escaped from enslavement in Connecticut and Rhode Island. After their names and circumstances were recorded in the *Book of Negroes*, they travelled to Shelburne with their five-month old daughter Fanny in the fall of 1783. This historic record allowed Brueggergosman's family story to reach back over six generations. The testing of her brother Neville's Y-DNA stretched her family's origins back even further. The genetic analysis indicated that her paternal African ancestors were the Bassa of Cameroon. Interestingly enough, this Bantu-speaking people were noted for their musical abilities.

The Legacy of Black Loyalists in Africa

(1792 – PRESENT)

Given that the majority of Loyalist refugees settled in what is now Canada, one can be forgiven for thinking that we are the only country where historically minded descendants celebrate the contributions of their loyal ancestors. However, since 1859, people in Sierra Leone have been commemorating the legacy that they have inherited as descendants of Black Loyalists.

Not unlike the Black Loyalist Heritage Society, the Nova Scotia and Maroon Descendants Association of Sierra Leone collects genealogical information on their Black Loyalist ancestors and remembers the struggles of Loyalist settlement.

Those who can trace their ancestors back to Black Loyalists traditionally refer to their forebears as Nova Scotians. However, even though they do not use the word *Loyalists*, they know that faithfulness to King George III was a hallmark of "the Nova Scotians" and remember their contributions to the British war effort during the American Revolution.

When the association wrote to Queen Victoria in 1862, they noted that their membership had "that same loyalty and devotion as animated our fathers when they fought and bled for your Majesty's Illustrious Grandsire, King George of imperishable memory, in the War of American Independence." To be in Sierra Leone and to have an ancestor who once lived in Nova Scotia was, *ipso facto*, to be a Black Loyalist descendant.

So proud were the "Nova Scotians" (or "Settlers") of their Loyalist heritage, they were able to maintain a separate identity within their country into the late nineteenth century and beyond. Census records for Sierra Leone list the Nova Scotians as a separate ethnic group from 1792 until the 1870s.

Today, Black Loyalists' descendants make up a component of the Krio population of Sierra Leone. This ethnic group also includes the descendants of the Maroons, England's Black poor and the Recaptives (Africans rescued from slave ships). Their heritage, as demonstrated in traditions, clothing, language and lifestyle, is a mixture of a variety of cultures.

Nevertheless, the values brought to Sierra Leone by Black Loyalists were foundational for Krio society. A walk through Freetown in the nineteenth century would demonstrate their influence in architectural styles (southern colonial, two-storeyed with shingles), in street and business names that originated in the *Book of Negroes* ledger, in a grammar and pronunciation that reflected the southern colonies and in the style of clothing once common in Nova Scotia. Black Loyalists were responsible for bringing Christianity to the country, including the Lady Huntingdon's Connexion, an obscure denomination that once had a congregation in Birchtown.

Cassandra Garber, a leader in the Krio Descendants Union, feels that the Freetown settlement thrived in the

1790s due to the hard lessons Black Loyalists learned from the trials and tribulations that they experienced in Nova Scotia. "They had the temperament to make a success of the settlement." The Black Loyalists came as family units and brought positive aspects of the Western world with them.

Nova Scotia's loss was definitely Sierra Leone's gain. The 1792 exodus resulted in the Maritime Black Loyalist communities losing most of their clergymen, teachers and political leaders as well as a significant portion of the colonies' work force.

Chief among those leaders was Thomas Peters. Had it not been for him, there would have been no new African homeland for Black Loyalists. However, Peters's expectation that Sierra Leone would be a colony governed by its free Black settlers conflicted with the plans of the Sierra Leone Company. He led the opposition to the proposed operation of the colony but died within months of the Black Loyalists' arrival. Nevertheless, Peters is remembered as a courageous opponent of injustice and discrimination.

Despite the difficulties surrounding its first years of settlement, Freetown showed the previously untapped potential of Black Loyalists. In addition to several retail stores, a printing press, a church, a school and a library, Freetown had a fishing port, a justice of the peace, a constabulary and two open spaces for public gatherings. The settlement boasted twelve streets with a view of the shore that could be seen from the timber-frame houses of the settlers — a far cry from any Black Loyalist settlement in the Maritimes.

While the community had only 400 households, its political campaigns had all of the trappings of twenty-first century elections. Placards were posted in public venues, heartfelt speeches caused crowds to gather and some sermons contained endorsements for particular candidates. The women of Sierra Leone were the first of their sex to vote in elections anywhere in the world. Magistrates and judges were elected offices; juries of peers decided the fate of those charged with crimes. These are amazing political developments for the late eighteenth

century, but they grew out of Black Loyalists' profound belief that they were "free British subjects and expect to be treated as such."

Like its Canadian counterpart, the Nova Scotia and Maroon Descendants Association has a number of important genealogical records for the descendants of the eighty-two Black Loyalist families who were Sierra Leone's founders. Up until 1952, the association held regular cultural nights in Freetown, the country's capital. Historian James W. St. Walker recalled meeting a proud "Settler" woman who told him about dances and songs from Nova Scotia.

"When our people came here they had their own food, their own language, their own religion, their own culture . . . We all dressed up in the old Nova Scotian costumes. We women wore long dresses with our breasts pushed up high and a tight girdle and a bustle out the back. Our shoes had buckles and we wore high lacy collars. We wore mittens, not gloves, and carried umbrellas, and had big hats on our heads."

Walker quoted Black Loyalist descendants in Sierra Leone as saying, "Family is everything for us", "The Nova Scotians are different" and "The church is the solid rock for all Nova Scotian people. Nova Scotians in Freetown today have kept alive their forbears' fundamental concerns for freedom and self-determination . . ."

Being of Black Loyalist or Nova Scotian descent means more than being able to trace a bloodline or donning the colourful clothing of loyal refugees. Reflecting on the values of their ancestors, modern Sierra Leoneans told Walker:

"We came here to be free. The Nova Scotian must be free . . . This was a free country, and it belonged to the Nova Scotians. Then the colonial people came. They ruined it for us, and they betrayed their own queen. Queen Victoria gave us a charter for our land and our freedoms. But the colonial people refused to give us all the land we were promised, and even took away what we had."

Like the Black Loyalist settlers of the Maritimes and Upper Canada who sought compensation from the

British government, the "Nova Scotians" of Sierra Leone could also look back on a history of land wrongfully seized and lost.

The association faded after the 1950s, but Sierra Leone's founding fathers and mothers were still remembered with annual events that celebrated the arrival of the fifteen ships from Nova Scotia in 1792. The latter included a parade to the fleet's landing place and a religious service held under Freetown's landmark cotton tree. Two centuries earlier, almost 1,200 Black Loyalists celebrated their safe journey across the Atlantic from Nova Scotia beneath this same tree.

With the dawn of the twenty-first century, interest in the Black Loyalist heritage of Sierra Leone has enjoyed a revival, and since 2014, a revived Nova Scotia and Maroon Descendants Association now hosts its own Facebook page. As its home page indicates,

"The current effort is a revival of the Association that existed during the nineteenth and twentieth centuries, and is for the purpose of celebrating the Nova Scotian Settlers and the Jamaican Maroons, two of the founding populations of pre-colonial Freetown . . . the aim of this page is to highlight the history, culture, and descendants of the Nova Scotian Settlers and the Maroons."

Thus Black Loyalist history is remembered and celebrated in Sierra Leone.

The Maroons

The Maroons were 600 people of African descent who were deported from Jamaica to Halifax, Nova Scotia in 1796. The refortification of Citadel Hill and the foundations of Government House are two architectural reminders of the Maroons' contributions to the capital area. Unhappy in Nova Scotia, the Jamaicans successfully petitioned the government for resettlement in Sierra Leone in 1800.

Armorial Bearings

The Black Loyalist Heritage Society Board of Directors initiated the idea of armorial bearings in 2003. They applied to the Canadian Heraldic Authority, under the powers held by the former Governor General of Canada, The Right Honourable Adrienne Clarkson, for petition for Armorial Bearings. The BLHS is the first Black heritage organization that has received Armorial Bearings, granted and recorded in the Public Register of Arms, Flags and Badges of Canada on March 15th, 2006.

Original concept by Darrel E. Kennedy, Assiniboine Herald, assisted by the Heralds of the Canadian Heraldic Authority. Painter: Linda Nicholson.

Symbolism of the Armorial Bearings

Arms: The appearance of the shield portrays directly the nature and purpose of the Black Loyalist Heritage Society. The shield background is black. Loyalist civil coronets allude to the vast majority of people fleeing on fleets of ships who were non-combatants. The ship's wheel is taken from the emblem in use for some time, and represents the ships bringing settlers to their new homes. On one hand, the wheel represents the past, alluding to the ships landing in 1783. On the other hand, it represents the present, alluding to the society's role of community development, with various interests meeting together and steering toward a goal.

Crest: The lion and the coronet represent the soldiers under the banner of the Crown whose actions allowed the people to settle in Nova Scotia. The anchor alludes to the sacrifice of the families that required them to raise anchor in their previous home and set down in their home. The mantling has apparent footprints symbolizing the trek the settlers had to make.

Motto: *The Heart of Your Knowledge is in Your Roots* speaks to the interest in heritage displayed by society members.

Supporters: The lions, symbol of the pride of Africa, demonstrate courage, since the people needed that quality to face the hardships and to start a new life. The two coronets are shown red and green, which together with black and gold, are the colours of Africa. Each coronet can represent new life emerging from sacrifice. The rock is the land area around Birchtown where the settlers landed in Nova Scotia, represented by the provincial flower — the mayflower.

Flag: The flag is a banner of the arms, meaning that the symbols of the shield represent themselves in a square form.

Badge: The Loyalist settlers, represented by the coronet, found a location at Birchtown, marked their spot and now this location in Nova Scotia is memorialized by the saltire pattern.

FOR FURTHER READING

Black Loyalists: Southern Settlers of Nova Scotia's First Free Black Communities by Ruth Holmes Whitehead, Nimbus Publishing, Ltd, Halifax, NS, 2013

The Blacks in Canada: A History by Robin W. Winks, Yale University Press, London, UK, 1971

The Black Loyalists: The Search for a Promised Land in Nova Scotia and Sierra Leone, 1783-1870 by James W. St. G. Walker, University of Toronto Press, Toronto, ON, 2017

Black Patriots and Loyalists: Fighting for Emancipation in the War for Independence by Alan Gilbert, the University of Chicago Press, Chicago, IL, 2012

Bury the Chains: Prophets and Rebels in the Fight to Free an Empire's Slaves by Adam Hochschild, Mariner Books, New York, NY, 2006

Epic Journeys of Freedom: Runaway Slaves of the American Revolution and Their Global Quest for Liberty by Cassandra Pybus, Beacon Press, Boston, MA, 2006

Liberty's Exiles: American Loyalists in the Revolutionary World by Maya Jasanoff, Alfred A. Knopf, New York, NY, 2011

Loyalists and Layabouts: The Rapid Rise and Faster Fall of Shelburne, Nova Scotia by Stephen Kimber, Anchor Canada, 2009

North to Bondage: Loyalist Slavery in the Maritimes by Harvey Amani Whitfield, University British Columbia Press, Vancouver, BC, 2016

The Other Loyalists: Ordinary People, Royalism, and the Revolution in the Middle Colonies, 1763-1787 edited by Joseph S. Tiedemann, Eugene R. Fingerhut and Robert W. Venables, State University of New York, Albany, NY, 2009

Rough Crossings: The Slaves, the British, and the American Revolution by Simon Schama, Penguin Group, Toronto, ON, 2007

INDEX